August Postcards
A Poetry Collection

Constance Taylor

Fathom Publishing

Copyright © 2024 All rights reserved.
No part of this publication may be reproduced, distributed, or transmitted in any form or by any means, including photocopying, recording, or other electronic or mechanical methods, without the prior written permission of the publisher, except in the case of brief quotations embodied in critical reviews and certain other noncommercial uses permitted by copyright law.

ISBN 978-1-888215-89-2 paperback
ISBN 978-1-888215-33-5 ebook

Printed in United States

Cover and interior photos by Constance Taylor unless otherwise credited
Rubber Boots by Charlie Schwing
Walnut Branch by AJ Kubler
Lure by billiondigital/Depositphotos.com
Email Icon by djv/Depositphotos.com
Onions Rings by stocksolutions/Depositphotos.com
Music Font by Fontspace.com

Fathom Publishing Company
PO Box 200448 | Anchorage, AK 99520
FathomPublishing.com

Contents

Introduction	v
What's Blue?	1
Like a Dog with a Bone	2
Conch Shell	3
Out my Window	4
Out of Sight	5
Resilience	6
Waiting	7
Read a Poem to Me	8
Yesterday's Tea	9
Redpolls	10
Riding through the Night	11
Walnut Trees	12
Sleeping Cat	13
Accounting for Happiness	14
Ageless Woods	15
Favorite Toy	16
New Kitten	17
Alaska's Winter Sun	18
Trout's Viewpoint	19
Gurgling Waters	20
Spring	21
Unexpected	22
Forget-Me-Not	23

Onion Rings	24
Tomorrow	25
Technology's Daily Task	26
At the End	27
Poetry Opens Doors	28
Love Is Consideration	29
Cat on my Chest	30
Bigger Fish to Fry	31
Old Boots	32
About the Author	33

Introduction

A collection of thirty-one poems shared with Poetry Postcard Fest participants during the 2024 season.

Cascadia Poetics Lab sponsors the annual Poetry Postcard Fest every August. Register to participate in the next Poetry Postcard Fest at https://cascadiapoeticslab.org/poetrypostcards.

Constance Taylor
December 2024

What's Blue?

I look for blue today
and see it everywhere.
Steller's jay flying past,
kingfisher perched above,
damselfly resting in the bush,
robin eggs in nearby nest,
don't ignore me, peacock,
bluebells at my feet,
iris, lupine, morning glory,
shining bright.

Like a Dog with a Bone

It keeps me company when I'm all alone
but always, always I should have known
never agreed to put it on a throne.

I should have seen the danger, should have flown
but now I know that it's too late and groan,
my cell phone has me like a dog with a bone.

Conch Shell

walking the beach in dream mode,
I came upon a conch shell, perfect
in coil and color, held it
in my hand and put it to my ear
to hear the ocean roar.

Out my Window

Chickadees
    chirping
        chittering
            chattering
                cheekily fussing
                    with each other.

Out of Sight

I see nothing happening
on the snow-covered hillside
but sight deceives me.

As life prepares for spring,
the garden voles feast
in the buried compost pile
and scurry through the hedge.

Resilience

stand by the river
feel the cool waters

flowing from the mountains
carrying tiny bits to the sea

nourishing the ocean waters
witness earth's resilience.

Waiting

waiting for the taxi by the mailbox,
woodpeckers pound on the tree
where peanut butter is hidden.

hoverflies seek pollen in the spirea bushes
where a spider spins a web
for the tiny swarming no-see'ems.

I remember the times
these small mosquito-like critters
bit my arms and cheer
for the diligent spider.

Read a Poem to Me

let me hear your voice
as the words ring clear,
take me to another place.

I'll close my eyes
and see more clearly
as words become a melody
that sounds so lovely in my ear.

we'll stop a moment now,
then read it once again.

Yesterday's Tea

each day a new ending
as setting sun eases from my view
over distant mountain peaks.

each day a new beginning
as morning sun peeks over the horizon
never at the same spot
between the birch trees.

I try to start each day anew
discarding yesterday's frustrations
as I pour out yesterday's tea
boiling water for a fresh pot.

Redpolls

a dozen redpolls cavort
chirping and fighting
seeking sunflower seeds
in the freshly fallen snow.

flitting hither and thither
never happy in a single spot
always the next is greener.

could that be me, always seeking,
never in one spot long enough
to find the treasure there.

Riding through the Night

The radio was my nightly friend
as I clustered closely by to hear
Lone Ranger's cry Hi Ho, Silver
as they raced across wild lands.

Silver led my eager dreams
as we raced through sage brush high.

I miss those long-lost nights
and wish again to hear the Ranger's cry.

Walnut Trees

I was a child the day my father
pruned the walnut trees.

"Trim every branch
that grows downward from the limb."

He did not say; I did not think until today
there is a message here for life.

Trim thoughts that lead away from light
for as you think of darkness, darkness grows.

Turn to the sun, seek light,
the harvest will be sweet.

Sleeping Cat

The cat curls in sleep beside me.
A warm spot at my back that signals
all our world is quiet now. No enemy
near to threaten those at rest.

And so I close my eyes
and shut my ears to noise
and let my body functions slow.

Past days worries slip away along
with tomorrow's imagined woes.

Accounting for Happiness

Happiness comes unannounced,
unsought, a welcome surprise
when you open your heart
to let it in.

But first
there is a price to pay.
Relinquish selfish thoughts
or happiness cannot not abide.

Ageless Woods

Deep red bark of the madrone
smooth as I run my hand along the limb.

Peeling strips of eucalyptus
reveal fresh colors as with length.

White gleam of birch accents
black lines and pale orange glow.

Rough crinkled spruce displays
all shades of black and brown.

I walk through ageless woods,
overcome.

Favorite Toy

flopping fish don't fool me,
fake mice not for me,
stuffed birds not my thing.

toilet paper roll
now here's a toy
I can really get my paws
around.

New Kitten

elderly cat growls as
new kitten in the house
interrupts her rest,

takes her treats,
usurps her toys,
plays with her humans.

but wait, it is nice
to cuddle close
on cold evenings.

Alaska's Winter Sun

the precious hours
when its glowing globe
hangs over the distant horizon
grow shorter every day.

as darkness claims
each passing day, I wonder
will darkness conquer all
or will my days grow long again.

Trout's Viewpoint

stream water cool and clear
golden leaves of fall are near
bugs and flies hiding here.

bright colors catch my eye
I spy a big one floating by
and lunge to clasp it tight
to find I'm in a terrible plight.

Gurgling Waters

I still remember walking,
walking along the creek, hearing.

hearing gurgling waters tumbling,
tumbling over stones, gravity pulling.

pulling droplets downhill as if rushing,
rushing to join the ocean, hastening.

hastening to mix with salt water's racing,
racing waves part of the constant cycling.

cycling of earth's waters through sky,
sky and cloud to earth again.

Spring

Potter Marsh in springtime is alive with the arrival of migrating birds: the loud honking of Canada geese, the snow-white beauty of trumpeter swans, and the excitement of fast-moving diving Arctic terns. The last of winter's ice melts as the long days of northern sun return. Life's adventures play out. Dragonflies pursue mosquitoes perhaps unaware Arctic terns are hunting dragonflies to feed their hatchlings.

>spring in the marshlands
>life, growth, hunger abounds
>danger lurks close

Unexpected

I watch out my window
as the woodpecker gathers
peanuts to take to his nest
he's perched on the feeder.

it's over in a second
today it is the hawk
who will bring
food to his young.

Forget-Me-Not

blue on forest floor
spring flowers beside a log
say forget-me-not

    forest color gleaming
    blue flowers grace a stump
    say forget-me-not

        summer is our time
        as winter snows start to fall
        say forget-me-not

Onion Rings

careful cutting
circles drop in boiling oil
crisp greasy goodness

Tomorrow

I thought there would always be
tomorrow and tomorrow after,
again, and again, never ending.

summer vacations marked years,
winter holidays divided winters,
and always there was tomorrow.

thirty thousand tomorrows bring
realization—days are not infinite,
a reminder to live in today.

Technology's Daily Task

morning emails bloom again
sort out those from friends, delete the rest.

some email masquerade,
dear friend they start to fool you to read on.

you'll find they have a sale for you, a loan make,
or perhaps a medicine you should take.

and still each morning, I participate,
hoping that the email I ignore as spam
did not come from my best friend.

At the End

I look around the room
knowing I must leave
to pass into the darkness
of an unknown future.

what is left behind?

only what was shared with others,
the kind word spoken on the air
lives beyond the darkness
into the forever future.

Poetry Opens Doors

unbidden thoughts revealed
by freely-typing fingers
insight into past events
not recognized 'til now
joy in crafting words
bringing understanding.

Love Is Consideration

dishes in the sink
    wipe the counter off
dirty clothes in the hamper
    not the floor
shoes on in rack
    not the doorway
it's small things
that can speak
    and be heard
larger than words.

Cat on my Chest

a note to the cat who sits
contentedly on my chest
between my eyes and book.

do you think you are transparent?
perhaps that your visit takes
priority? No, I think you wish
to urge me to the kitchen and
the treat you know you merit.

your paws kneed as your teeth
nibble my fingers. Do you remember
your long-past kitten days
when you were just a ball of fur?

Bigger Fish to Fry

I'm glad I'm just a little guy,
he must have bigger fish to fry.

I must be never tempted by the fly
that dangles by my watchful eye.

I'm sorely tempted and I worry as I try
to keep my hunger in abeyance and not comply
as my body urges me to grab the lure
that dangles so closely by.

Old Boots

bright orange, knee-high, ridged sole,
old rubber boots that sit in the corner
of old memory.

do they miss the old days when we fished together
and they steadied my grip on the rolling deck
or are they content to rest alone with memories?

About the Author

Constance Taylor left California to become a commercial fisherman in Alaska in the 1960s. She fished salmon, crab, and shrimp for twenty years in Prince William Sound. Constance then settled in Cordova to become a printer and art gallery owner. She moved to Anchorage in the 1990s to work as a paralegal, auctioneer, and bookkeeping consultant. Now she's a photographer, publisher, and author.

Her children's books include *Midnight on the Alaska Highway, Growing up in Alaska: A Baby Arctic Tern,* and *Sik-Sik: An Arctic Ground Squirrel.*

Her poetry has appeared in *Alaska Women Speak, Litmore Literary Magazine,* and *Lobardi Voices.*

https://www.fathomtwist.com/

www.ingramcontent.com/pod-product-compliance
Lightning Source LLC
Chambersburg PA
CBHW050209130526
44590CB00043B/3366